THE HEL^{3}P METHOD

THE HELP^3 METHOD

A Guide to Supporting Little Hurting Hearts Through Grief

BRADLEY VINSON

VINSON CREATIVE PUBLISHING
2024

The HELP Method:
A Guide to Supporting Little Hurting Hearts Through Grief

For information, contact
VC Publishing
PO Box 536
Argyle, TX 76226
info@vinsoncs.com

ISBN: 978-0-9894976-8-8

Printed in the United States of America

First Edition

DEDICATION

To my grandsons,

For years, I've done my best to be an example of how to grieve in a healthy way, even though I know I've fallen short at times. I'm really thankful for your patience and love as I try to be the best version of myself for you.

TABLE OF CONTENTS

THE ROLE OF THIS BOOK

This book is designed to assist caring adults in understanding and supporting grieving children through insights, real-life examples, and actionable advice. **However, I need to emphasize that this book is not a substitute for professional counseling or grief coaching.**

Grief is a profoundly personal and delicate process. While the information provided here can be helpful, it may not address all the specific challenges of an individual's grief journey. Professional counselors and grief coaches are trained to deal with a wide range of issues associated with grief, and they can offer personalized support and strategies tailored to the specific needs of both you "the caregiver," and your child. If you want to explore some options, visit BradleyVinson.com for more information.

If you find yourself overwhelmed or if the child shows signs of prolonged or intense grief, I recommend that you seek professional help.

Remember, seeking professional help is a sign of strength and responsibility. It demonstrates a commitment to the well-being of yourself and the child. Grief can sometimes bring unexpected challenges, and having a professional guide can make a difference in the healing journey.

As a caregiver, your well-being is equally as important. Supporting a grieving child can be emotionally taxing, and you need to have a support system in place for yourself.

Use this book as a starting point, a guide to better understand and support the grieving child in your care. Let it empower you with knowledge and strategies. Embrace the grief journey with compassion, patience, and the willingness to seek professional support when necessary. With the right tools and support, you can navigate this challenging path and foster healing and resilience in the face of loss.

Be encouraged on this hardest of journeys.

INTRODUCTION

Creating The HEL³P Method was not an academic exercise but part of my journey toward healing. It began with the death of my four-year-old granddaughter, Alanna, an event that shook the foundations of our family. In the wake of this heartbreak, my wife and I found ourselves in the roles of caregivers of Alanna's brothers, ages two and six at the time.

The depth of their grief at such tender ages was overwhelming, and I often felt lost—searching for tools and resources to guide my family through this dark valley. It was a journey that none of us were prepared for, yet one we had to travel together.

Through the days of shared tears, quiet moments of remembrance, and the many questions that sprang from my grandsons' young minds and little hurting hearts, I started to piece together what would become a roadmap for us—The HEL³P Method. These were not just abstract concepts but real, tangible tools born out of our day-to-day experiences and my affinity for acronyms.

Each letter of HEL³P – **Have the Hard and Honest Conversations, Express Yourself, Lean in, Love More, Let Them Lead Sometimes, and Have Patience**—became a foundation that supported not only my grandsons but also my wife and me as we attempted to provide the care and understanding they needed.

It became clear that what we were learning could support other caring adults in the difficult position of nurturing little hurting hearts. The HEL³P Method culminates these lived experiences, insights gained, and love shared.

This book is more than just a guide; it is a testament to resilience, the enduring power of love, and the capacity for healing even in the youngest among us. If you are reading this, perhaps facing the difficult task of caring for a grieving child, I hope that the tools and insights within these pages offer you the same support, guidance, and comfort that they brought to my family. May this guide be a companion to you as you walk alongside those little hurting hearts, helping them find their way back to light and hope.

H

HAVE THE HARD AND HONEST CONVERSATIONS

One of the most important ways to support children in their grief journey is through hard and honest conversations. Children, like adults, need truth to navigate their emotions effectively, but the "level" of truth we share should be tailored to their developmental stage.

Children process information and emotions differently at various ages. Younger children, aged 3-6, often think in concrete terms and might not grasp the permanence of death. I call this "matter-of-fact thinking." This thinking can also give caregivers a false impression of resilience. It can appear that your child is taking the loss "well" when, in fact, they are just taking in all the information given at face value.

School-aged children aged 7-12 start understanding finality but might struggle with abstract concepts like the soul or Heaven. Teenagers, meanwhile, can grapple with complex emotions and abstract ideas, much like adults, but are also in a stage where emotional regulation is still developing.

Honest conversations help children develop a realistic understanding of death and loss. They learn to trust adults and feel safer expressing their feelings. By keeping conversations age-appropriate, we respect their developmental stage and protect their emotional health.

TAKING ACTION

For Young Children (Ages 3-6):

- Use simple, straightforward language. Avoid metaphors that can be misunderstood. Script: "I have something sad to tell you. Grandma died, which means we won't see her anymore. It's okay to feel sad or confused."

For School-Aged Children (Ages 7-12):

- Be honest about the permanence of death but provide reassurance about continued care and love. Script: "I need to share something difficult. Your uncle has died. This means he won't be with us like he used to be. It's hard, and it hurts, and it's okay to feel whatever you're feeling, and you can tell us how you feel."

For Teenagers:

- Engage in open, honest conversations acknowledging the complexity of emotions. Be prepared for a range of reactions. Script: "I have some very sad news. Your cousin has passed away. This might bring up a lot of different feelings, and I'm here to talk about all of it whenever you're ready."

In all conversations, make sure to:

- Provide space for questions and express that all feelings are valid.
- Reassure them of the continuous presence and support in their lives.
- Adjust your approach based on your child's reactions and questions.

Honest conversations, while challenging, are important in helping children navigate grief. These conversations foster trust, understanding, and some emotional resilience, guiding children through one of life's toughest experiences.

I cannot over-emphasize the importance of stating the permanency of death, regardless of age. We have to speak the truth of the loss. Your blunt honesty, though painful, can reassure your child of what's going on and that you'll be there to help them through it.

Remember, just because you tell them, don't mistake hearing what you said as understanding it.

ROLE-PLAYING SCENARIOS

One effective way to prepare for difficult conversations about death with your child is through role-playing. This practice helps you anticipate and navigate the potential landmines in such discussions. Imagine a scenario where you can practice explaining the concept of death to your child. You could get comfortable using age-appropriate language, like, "When someone dies, their body stops working, and they don't feel any pain." You might also prepare for typical questions your child might ask, such as, "Where do people go when they die?" or "Will I see them again?"

In these role-play exercises, balancing honesty and sensitivity is critical, ensuring your child feels heard and comforted. Practicing these conversations in advance can help you feel more confident and equipped to handle real-life situations with compassion and clarity.

The first task I had in caring for my grieving grandsons was to start their grief journey through a hard and honest conversation. It was VERY difficult. Not long after I received the news that my granddaughter passed away in an accident, I had to drive nearly six hours to the scene (her school); it was then that the school principal told me, "Alanna's [older] brother doesn't know what happened, and I feel it's only right that you tell him." They prepared a little room for us and went to get him from his class. I met him in the hallway on shaky legs. He knew "something" was different about this visit. I walked him into that room to have the "hard and honest" conversation about his sister. I had to tell him she was never coming back home. He looked me in the eye and asked if he could hug her again. I had to say I didn't know. I didn't have the heart at that moment to say no. Then he said, "Thank you, PawPaw, for telling me," and gave me a big hug. We sat and cried together for the next ten minutes.

I cannot sugarcoat it; that's probably my hardest conversation. I've given bad news to people before, fired people, notified family members of deaths, and more, but that ripped my heart out. You may find yourself in that same position, where you are the person responsible for starting the grief journey of a child you are caring for. It is no easy task, but you can do it. Prepare for the opportunity.

REFLECTIVE EXERCISE

Role-play a conversation with your child about loss using age-appropriate language. Record your thoughts and feelings during this exercise.

SELF-ASSESSMENT QUESTIONS

How comfortable do I feel discussing the topic of death with my child?

What are my beliefs about death, and how might these impact the conversation?

Can I think of ways to simplify complex concepts about grief for different age groups?

How would I handle emotional responses when talking about death with my child?

What strategies can I use to ensure I am being transparent and honest in these conversations?

How can I better prepare myself to answer unexpected or difficult questions my child might ask about death?

JOURNALING PROMPTS

- Write about a time you had to discuss a complex topic with your child. How did it go?

- Reflect on how your childhood experiences with grief have shaped your approach to these conversations.

NOTES/IDEAS

E

EXPRESS YOURSELF

Children often look to the adults in their lives for examples of expressing and coping with their emotions. Children see and copy our behavior, especially regarding emotional expression and coping mechanisms. I often use the adage that dads and other father figures are not the thermometers in the home; they are the thermostats. Simply put, we adults create the atmosphere/temperature in our environments, and when it comes to grief, it's more important than most realize. How we express our grief can affect the grieving journey of the children we are caring for.

It's about showing emotions and how we manage and communicate them. When we model healthy expressions of grief, children learn it's okay to feel sad, cry, talk about their loss, and continue living and finding moments of happiness. Our children should see us grieve healthily. Save the deep, gut-wrenching, soul-cleansing cries for your private time. I'm not saying hide your grief from the child you are caring for, but there is a fine line between setting an example and putting your child in a position of fear for your well-being.

We must ensure that the child we care for does not feel they need to be our comforter/caretaker/counselor. That is not their role! We must also preserve and defend their right to be a child. Sometimes, children can find themselves in a "have to grow up now" situation due to loss. That's a real possibility, but we should not facilitate it if it's not part of their journey.

TAKING ACTION

- **Be Open About Your Emotions:** Let your child see that you are sad and that it's a normal response to loss. However, you should also demonstrate healthy ways to cope and continue with daily life.

- **Find Healthy Outlets:** Encourage journaling, creating art, or engaging in prayer or meditation. These activities can help you process emotions in a nonverbal yet expressive way.

- **Share Your Coping tools for healing:** Talk about how you manage grief. Whether talking to friends, engaging in physical activities, or seeking professional help, sharing these strategies can help children find the proper coping methods.

- **Create a Safe Space for Expression:** Encourage children to express their grief in their own way. Validate their feelings and provide them with tools for expression, like drawing, writing, or simply talking.

- **Balance Grief with Normalcy:** While it's important to grieve, it's also essential to continue with routine activities. This balance shows children that life does move forward, even in the face of loss, and that it's okay to find moments of joy amid sadness.

By expressing yourself in a healthy and balanced way, you provide a powerful model for grieving children. This approach helps them understand and express their grief and teaches them valuable coping skills they can use throughout their lives.

> Remember, they are children, not your counselors. Sometimes, we need to shelter them from our grief—not hide it entirely, but it shouldn't be the predominant thing they see from us.

Many times throughout the early months of our journey, my grandsons would randomly ask, "Are you thinking about Alanna?" "Are you sad?" and similar sentiments. I realized these were openings for discussions and validating feelings to speak about grief and the grieving process. I would say, "Yes, I'm thinking about Alanna," even if I wasn't sometimes, and their immediate response was usually, "I am too." I would affirm feeling sad, and the boys would acknowledge their sadness and start conversations about how we all could work through it.

PRACTICAL EXAMPLES

Journaling and Memory Boxes: Journaling offers a space to pour out thoughts and feelings, helping everyone process their emotions at their own pace. It can be helpful for those who might find it hard to express their feelings verbally. Encourage writing letters to loved ones, recording memories, or simply expressing daily emotions related to the loss.

Memory boxes can be a tangible connection to the person who has passed. They can be filled with photos, mementos, or anything sentimental. For children, this might include drawings, toys, or a piece of clothing that reminds them of the person. Creating a memory box can be a family activity, allowing for shared expressions of grief and remembrance. These boxes can become cherished items that honor the loved one and serve as a tool for healing.

REFLECTIVE EXERCISE

Engage in an expressive activity like drawing or writing about your feelings of grief. Notice the emotions that surface during this process.

SELF-ASSESSMENT QUESTIONS

Do I feel I have healthy outlets for expressing my grief?

How do I usually express my emotions, and are there other methods I might find helpful?

How do my expressions of grief influence the children around me?

What emotions do I find most challenging to express, and why?

How can I model healthy emotional expression to my child during the grieving process?

JOURNALING PROMPTS

- Journal about a day in your grief journey, noting the ups and downs.

- Write a note or letter to the person you lost, expressing everything you wish to say.

NOTES/IDEAS

13

LEAN IN, LOVE MORE

In the wake of loss, your child can feel a heavy sense of insecurity and uncertainty. One of the most effective ways to address these feelings is through increased physical affection and a consistent, reassuring presence (Lean In and Love More). Physical touch and emotional availability can help your child feel safe and loved, especially during distress. Physical affection releases the "love hormone," which can reduce stress and promote calm and connection. In the context of grief, this becomes even more critical as children navigate the rough waters of loss.

> In my experience, my grandsons wanted and still want to be in my space a lot. I believe some of this is due to grief. More hugs and the need to know where I am, where I'm going, and for how long all stem from the need for security and connection that their grief experience has bruised.

TAKING ACTION

- **Increase Physical Affection:** Hugs, holding hands, or a comforting touch can provide much-needed comfort. Be mindful of your child's comfort level with physical affection and adjust as needed.

- **Create New Rituals:** Establish new routines that foster connection. This could be a nightly story, a regular walk in the park, or a weekly family movie night. The consistency of these rituals provides stability and comfort.

- **Be Emotionally Available:** Be physically present but also emotionally available. Listen when they want to talk, comfort them when upset, and offer your presence as a steady, comforting force.

- **Regular Check-Ins:** Set aside specific times for check-ins. This could be a daily time when you sit together and talk about how everyone feels without distractions.

- **Be Present for Important Moments:** Be there for special moments like anniversaries or birthdays of the lost loved one. Your presence at these times shows your commitment to sharing in the grief and the healing process.

Incorporating these increased physical affection and presence practices can significantly aid your child's grieving process. It reassures them that they are not alone, provides a sense of safety and stability, and shows your support and love, all crucial in navigating the complexities of grief and loss.

PRACTICAL EXAMPLE

Family Activities to Promote Closeness: Family dinners, walks, or participating in a shared hobby can enhance a sense of togetherness and understanding.

These activities don't have to be elaborate; the key is their regularity and the sense of security they provide. For instance, a weekly family dinner where everyone shares something about their week can create a routine that children look forward to. Walking together can offer a peaceful setting for conversations or shared silence. In these moments, family members can find comfort, reminding each other that they are not alone in their grief and you are all participating in loving each other through it.

It's not always about finding the right thing to say or do, but often just about being there, offering a shoulder to lean on, and a comforting presence during pain.

REFLECTIVE EXERCISE

- Plan and follow through with a family bonding activity. Note the reactions and interactions during this time.

SELF-ASSESSMENT QUESTIONS

How often do I engage in activities promoting closeness with the child I care for?

What new activities can I introduce that might help us connect more deeply?

How do I respond to my child's need for affection and emotional support during times of grief?

What barriers, if any, do I face in providing physical comfort and reassurance to my grieving child?

How can I better recognize and respond to moments when my child needs extra love and attention?

JOURNALING PROMPTS

- Reflect on a cherished memory that involves a shared family activity.

- Write about how you have seen love and support expressed in your family during grief. (If not, reflect on how you hoped it would be.)

NOTES/IDEAS

13

LET THEM LEAD SOMETIMES

Each child's grieving process is unique and varies by age, personality, and the relationship they had with their deceased loved one. Allowing your child to lead or simply including them in decisions on how their loved one is honored and remembered respects their individuality and feelings. It helps them process their emotions in a way that is most natural and healing for them. This can lead to healthier long-term emotional outcomes and give them a sense of empowerment.

> All this came to a head when two impactful moments happened in our family. The first was when my oldest grandson asked if we could take out his sister's things and sit and talk about our memories of her—he was thinking about her and wanted us to take part and share stories. I don't know if I would have thought of that, especially to ask if everyone else wanted to join the activity. We got boxes of tissues, grabbed the storage bin with her things, and spent time reminiscing.

Second, one day, seemingly out of the blue, our grandson asked if we could talk about something, and then he said, "I don't like going to the cemetery as much as you (my wife and I) do. I'm okay with going on special occasions like holidays and birthdays, but I don't always like going. I know I don't have much of a choice. I'm a kid and know I cannot stay home alone, but I just wanted to tell you I don't like going as much as you do." We thanked him for his openness and for letting us know. We still include him and his brother for visits on special occasions but changed most of our visits to while they are at school during the day.

TAKING ACTION

- **Provide Options, Not Orders:** Present various ways to express grief, for example, art, writing, and talking, and let your child choose what feels right.

- **Conversation Starters:** Use open-ended questions to encourage expression. Ask, "Is there a special way you'd like to remember or honor [loved one]?" or "What do you need right now to feel heard and supported?"

- **Respect Their Choices:** If your child chooses a particular way to grieve or remember their loved one, support their decision, even if it's different from what you expected. If the choice feels a little "too much," be willing to bend a little and compromise.

- **Involve Them in Decisions:** When it comes to memorial services or anniversaries, involve your child in the planning. Ask for their input and honor their wishes as much as possible.

- **Regular Check-Ins:** Periodically check in with them to see their feelings and if their needs have changed.

By allowing your child to lead in their grieving process or, at minimum, have a voice in how the family group processes shared grief, we honor their individuality and support their emotional health. It's about providing guidance, respecting their ideas, creating an environment where they feel safe to grieve uniquely, and having a voice in the healing and memorial process.

PRACTICAL EXAMPLE

Child-Led Memorial Activities: One of the most empowering things we can do for a grieving child is to allow them to take the lead in how we all choose to remember and honor our loved ones who are no longer with us. This can be done by creating an open space for children to initiate or lead memorial activities. Encourage them to light a candle in memory of the person or assemble a photo collage that captures their favorite memories.

SELF-ASSESSMENT QUESTIONS

Do I tend to lead all the time when it comes to activities and discussions about grief with my child?

How can I create a safe and open environment that encourages my child to express their grief in their own way?

How comfortable am I with allowing my child to honor our loved one's life in ways different from mine?

What fears or concerns might I have about letting my child take the lead in memorial activities?

JOURNALING PROMPTS

- Journal about a time you let your child take the lead and how it felt.
- Write about what you have learned from your child's approach to grief and loss.

NOTES/IDEAS

P

HAVE PATIENCE

Grief in children, like adults, is a complicated and nonlinear process. It does not hold to a set timeline or predictable stages but instead ebbs and flows. Children may revisit their grief from different perspectives as they grow and their understanding of loss deepens. This unpredictable nature of grief requires us to have patience. Patience is vital in providing effective support and requires acknowledging your child's grief journey is unique and may take longer and different paths than expected.

Your child's grief will change over time as their maturity, awareness, and development change. Six-year-old grief differs from two-year-old grief, and twelve-year-old grief differs from six. Don't be surprised when "old" hurts come back as your child ages and recovery milestones are seemingly undone as their awareness and organic thought bring more questions or the loss is rehashed over and over. You must be willing to "circle back" and meet your child where they are in their grief.

TAKING ACTION

- **Recognize the Unpredictability of Grief:** Understand that grief can appear differently at different times. Be prepared for this and acknowledge it as a normal process.

- **Maintain Emotional Availability:** Continuously offer support, even if your child's grief seems to have subsided. Be ready to listen and provide comfort whenever your child revisits their grief.

- **Practice Mindfulness:** Engage in mindfulness exercises to cultivate patience. Deep breathing, prayer, or meditation can help manage your emotions and reactions.

- **Self-Care for the Caregiver:** Ensure you care for your emotional and physical well-being. A patient caregiver is well-rested, emotionally stable, and physically healthy.

- **Educate Yourself on Age-Appropriate Reactions:** Understand common grief reactions for different age groups. This knowledge can help set realistic expectations for how your child might respond at various stages.

- **Avoid Timelines for Grief:** Do not set expectations for how long grief should last. Be patient with the process, no matter how long it takes.

Patience in the face of your child's evolving grief is a powerful form of support. It allows children to feel safe and reassures them they have the time and space they need to heal.

Being in the position to witness the grief journeys of two of my four grandsons as they've grown through the developmental stages of a toddler to teen gives insight into how rough and tangled the journey can be for them and us.

Healing from and understanding grief is a process that cannot be rushed. It involves providing consistent care, understanding, and the right emotional environment at the right time.

Children's emotions and understanding of loss need time, love, and attention to heal. They also need caring adults willing to be wounded by old memories and emotions as they circle back to meet them where they are–no matter how far the adults have traveled on their own grief journeys.

REFLECTIVE EXERCISE

- Spend a day consciously practicing patience in all your interactions. Note the challenges and feelings that come.

SELF-ASSESSMENT QUESTIONS

How do I react when things don't progress as I expect in my grief journey or my child's?

What are some strategies I can use to build more patience?

What triggers impatience in me when dealing with my grieving child, and how can I address these triggers?

How do I react when my child's grieving process takes longer than I expected?

JOURNALING PROMPTS

- Write about a moment when patience led to a positive outcome in your grief journey.

- Reflect on when impatience has affected your ability to support your grieving child.

NOTES/IDEAS

FREQUENTLY ASKED QUESTIONS BY CAREGIVERS

How can I tell if my child's reaction to grief is typical or if they need professional help, and how long should I wait before seeking professional help? Each child's response to grief is unique, but sure signs can indicate the need for professional help. These include prolonged periods of depression, drastic behavior changes, withdrawal from activities they once enjoyed, or signs of extreme anxiety. If you're concerned, consulting with other professionals is always a good idea. If your child fell off their bike and broke their arm, how long would you wait to take them to the doctor to get it fixed? Now your child has a broken heart, how long do you think you should wait?

My child doesn't want to talk about their feelings. Should I be worried? Not necessarily. Children process grief in different ways. Some may feel uncomfortable expressing their feelings verbally and find other coping methods, such as through play or art. Encourage various forms of expression and be available if they choose to talk, but don't force conversations.

How do I balance my grief while trying to support my child? Balancing your grief with helping your child can be challenging. It's essential to take care of your own emotional needs, whether that means seeking support from friends, family, or professionals. Remember, put on your oxygen first. Showing your child that it's okay to grieve healthily and seek help can be a powerful lesson.

How soon should I return my child to their routine after a loss? The timeline can vary depending on the individual child and the nature of the loss. Pay attention to your child's behavior and emotions, and gradually return to routine activities, being flexible to adjustments as needed.

Is it okay to show my emotions and cry in front of my child? Yes, it's okay to show your feelings. It helps children understand that grieving is a natural process. It's also important to model healthy ways of coping with these emotions. This teaches children that while being sad is okay, there are ways to handle these feelings constructively.

My child seems to have moved on from the loss very quickly. Is this normal? Children sometimes appear to move on quickly, but this doesn't mean they've completed their grieving process. Remember that children may respond differently based on their level of understanding and development. They will revisit their grief as they grow older and their understanding deepens. Continuously offer support and check in with them.

How do I handle my child's questions about death and dying, and how do I explain the concept of death to a very young child? Answer their questions honestly but in a way that is appropriate for their age and maturity level. Provide reassurance and comfort, and be open to having ongoing conversations as their understanding evolves. Use straightforward language to explain death. Avoid euphemisms that can confuse them. Explain that when someone dies, their body stops working, and they won't be around the way they used to be. Reassure them with your presence and love.

Can younger children truly understand and process grief? Yes, even young children experience grief, though they may not understand or express it in the same way as older children or adults. It's essential to offer age-appropriate support and encourage expression through play or storytelling.

How can I help my child manage their anger about the loss and become more independent again? Acknowledge their anger as a valid part of the grieving process. Encourage them to express their anger healthily through physical activity or creative outlets. If the anger seems unmanageable, consider seeking help from a counselor. Clinginess is a common reaction to the fear of further loss. Gradually encourage independence by setting small, achievable goals for separation while ensuring consistent availability.

How can I help siblings who are grieving differently? Recognize and validate each child's unique way of grieving. Provide individual support based on their needs and encourage open communication within the family to foster understanding and empathy among siblings.

Should I take my child to the funeral or memorial service? This depends on the child's age, maturity, and willingness to attend. Discuss the event with them, explain what to expect, and let them decide. If they choose not to attend, find alternative ways to say goodbye or honor the deceased.

My child asks the same questions about death repeatedly. How should I handle this? Repeated questions can signify that your child is trying to understand and come to terms with the loss. Patiently answer their questions each time, as this repetition can be crucial to their processing.

I hope the answers clarified and guided your journey as a caregiver. Grief is a complex and personal experience, and it's natural to have more questions as you navigate this path.

For more information and resources, I invite you to visit my website at BradleyVinson.com. There, you'll find additional content to help you support your child and yourself through the grieving process.

Please contact me if you have any further questions or need personalized advice. I'd love to hear from you and assist however I can.

EMBRACING HOPE AND HEALING

I want to give you hope, practical wisdom, and spiritual encouragement. The journey you are on with your grieving child can be challenging, but it is also a pathway to profound growth and healing.

Remember that grief is a journey, not a destination. It's a winding path with its ups and downs. Applying the principles of **HEL^{3}P – Have the Hard and Honest Conversations, Express Yourself, Lean in, Love More, Let Them Lead Sometimes, and Have Patience** – equip yourself with practical tools to guide your child through this labyrinth of emotions. These tools are not just strategies but acts of love, understanding, and compassion that can make a significant difference in a young life reeling from loss.

Know that you are not alone in this journey. Many have walked this path before you, and many walk it with you now. Seek support when needed, lean on others, and never underestimate the power of a shared experience. Your role in your grieving child's life is invaluable. Your patience, understanding, and love are powerful forces that can help guide them back toward a place of peace and hope.

As you close this book, I pray that you carry forward the knowledge and strategies shared within these pages and the belief that your journey through grief will lead to healing, growth, and renewed joy in time.

May you find strength in your faith, hope in your journey, and love in every step you take with the child in your care.

APPLYING THE HEL³P METHOD IN YOUR JOURNEY

These "Next Steps" are designed to help you transition from understanding The HEL³P Method to actively applying it to supporting your grieving child. Use the principles of HEL³P in your daily life and interactions with your child experiencing grief.

STEP 1: REFLECT AND ASSESS

Start by reflecting on what you have learned from this book. Which aspects of The HEL³P Method resonated with you the most, and what parts don't quite fit where you are on your journey? Are there areas where you feel you need more understanding or practice? Assess your current situation with the grieving child or children in your care and identify specific areas where The HEL³P Method can be applied.

STEP 2: PLAN YOUR APPROACH

Based on your reflection, create a plan for how you will apply each element of HEL³P:

Have the Hard and Honest Conversations: Schedule an open conversation with your child, keeping their age and maturity in mind.

Express Yourself: Think of ways you can model healthy expressions of grief.

Lean in, Love More, and Let Them Lead Sometimes: Identify specific actions you can take to show more affection and support. Plan activities where your child can lead, expressing their grief. Be open to hearing them out about things they want to add and edit when planning how you memorialize your loved ones.

Have Patience: Remind yourself of the importance of patience and how you can practice it. Be willing and prepared to "Circle Back."

STEP 3: IMPLEMENT AND ADAPT

Put your plan into action. Remember, flexibility is critical. Be prepared to adapt your approach based on your child's responses and needs. Each child's grief journey is unique, and your support may need to evolve.

STEP 4: SEEK FEEDBACK AND COMMUNICATE

Engage in open communication with your child and, if proper, with other trusted adults or family members. Ask for feedback on the changes you have implemented.

STEP 5: CONTINUE YOUR EDUCATION

Grief care is an ongoing learning process. Consider joining support groups, attending workshops, or reading more. You can visit my website, BradleyVinson.com, for additional content and 1:1 coaching options for personalized insights on helping your child or you as you work through the healing process. The more you understand about grief, especially in your children, the better equipped you will be to provide adequate support.

STEP 6: PRACTICE SELF-CARE

Supporting a grieving child can be emotionally taxing. Ensure you are also taking care of your own emotional and physical well-being. It will make you a more effective caregiver.

STEP 7: CELEBRATE PROGRESS

Recognize and celebrate the progress both you and your child make. Even small steps in managing grief are significant. Celebrating these moments can encourage and build hope to continue the work required to heal healthily.

IMPORTANT NOTE: In my grandson's book, *What This Kid Wants Adults to Know About Grief*, he mentions he sometimes felt telling me about his grief would make me sad, and he didn't want to do that.

We have to be okay with not knowing some of the things going on with our children in their grief. Releasing the need to know everything for the sake of your child's healing is worth it. Remember, just like there are things you don't tell your children to not put unneeded burdens on them, they feel the same way about us.

I know it can be challenging, but build the strength to tell your child it's okay to talk to other [mutually] trusted adults about their grief. You have to be okay not being the only person your child talks with to feel better. It doesn't change your importance and their need for you.

Just being okay with it is not enough. You must tell them that; they must hear and understand you're okay with it.

HOW TO CONTACT BRADLEY

If you are interested in 1:1 coaching, training, or resources to support grieving children and families better, I can help. For more information about keynotes, training, workshops, and coaching, contact me:

Email: info@bradleyvinson.com
Website: www.bradleyvinson.com

To purchase bulk copies of this book at a discount for your organization, email me the subject line "bulk order inquiry," and I'll get back to you with details.

Thank you!

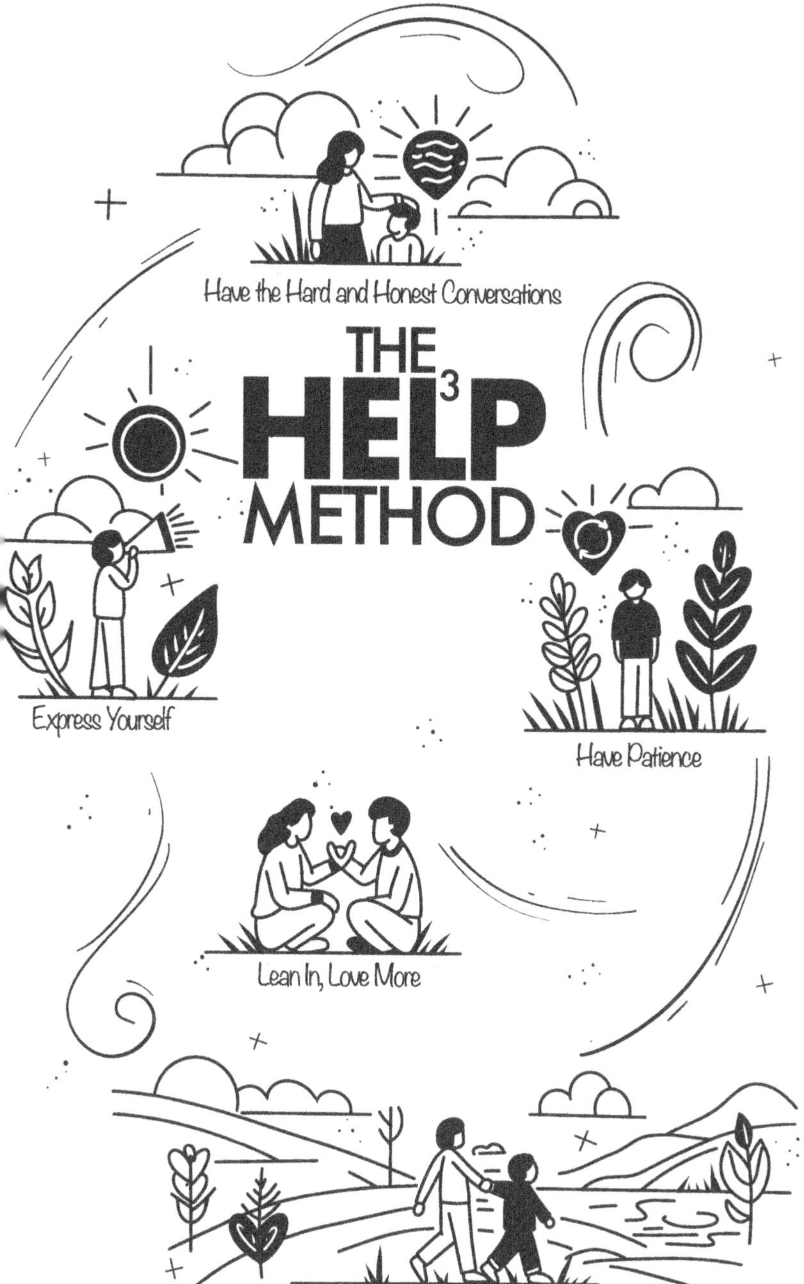
Have the Hard and Honest Conversations
THE
HELP
3
METHOD
Express Yourself
Have Patience
Lean In, Love More
Let Them Lead Sometimes

Made in the USA
Monee, IL
10 February 2025

11797834R00039